Foreword

It's summer in Tilda's garden, with bumblebees, whimsy cats, flowers, rabbits, frogs and dragonflies …

In this book you will find ideas on how to decorate both indoors and outdoors, and maybe you can get the summer feeling to start a little sooner and last a little longer.

A lazy summer day can be even nicer if you have a needlework project to work on. Sew what needs to be sewn on a sewing machine in advance, then pack everything else you need and some lunch and spend the day at the beach – bring some friends along too.

Many of the items can be used all year around, or you could adapt them with different colours and fabrics to fit another season better. You can, for example, sew red bird houses or change the garden angel's sun hat to a root thread wreath for Christmas. The bunnies can easily be changed to easter bunnies with just some pastel-coloured clothes. All the items featured are sewn, appliquéd and painted to the size of the patterns given at the back of the book, but you can easily enlarge the patterns on a photocopier.

Read about the different fabrics and materials used on page 4. There are a lot of different fabrics on the market and the assortment changes almost every day. It can therefore be hard to find exactly what you are looking for. Be open to alternatives to the fabrics you see used here, and maybe you will find something even better …

Wishing you a great summer!

Best regards,

Thanks to:
Dana Strandli, Mette Randem, Gro Stangeland, Torje and Matti, the girls at Lines Hobby, Boksenteret and Panduro Hobby for their collaboration. See Suppliers, page 64.

Contents

Materials

Fabrics

I have used a lot of single-coloured fabrics, many with a flaxy structure, and fabrics with classic squares and stripes. You can find good selections in any fabric shop. You can always cut up dishtowels, tablecloths and old clothes if you like the fabric or the pattern.

For skintones use warm beige or light brown fabrics. Do not use elastic fabrics, cotton fabric is preferred. Doll stockinette is not suitable for the patterns in this book, but can be used as a face patch on the bumblebees (see pages 14–15).

You can buy iron-on interfacing with adhesive on one side in fabric and craft shops.

Other

Different wreaths and pots can be found in craft shops, florists or garden centres. You can find smaller pots, small garden tools, metal wire, different shaped buttons, lolly sticks and natural materials like coconut fibre, wood fibre and root threads in craft shops.

Pots and watering cans with a flat back for the signs (pages 50–51) can be found at Panduro Hobby (see Suppliers, page 64).

The selection of fabrics and materials is changing all the time. If there is something in this book you can't find, be open to finding something to use instead, there are always good alternatives.

Reversing and stuffing

Make cuts in the seam allowance where the seams curve inwards, see example. Be careful that you don't cut the seams.

When you are reversing (turning out) the figure, use a stick or similar and be sure to reverse all the small details as well.

It is a good idea to iron the figure before you stuff it. You can use a stick to help you stuff the figure. To finish, close the opening by hand sewing it.

TONE FINNANGER

Crafting
Tilda's Friends

D&C
David and Charles

Tone Finnanger is an expert
in the fields of drawing,
shapes and colours, graphic
design and old paint
techniques. She worked as
an interior designer and
decorator in Oslo, Norway
before she moved to Tjøme
to open the shop Lines
Hobby in Tønsberg.

Other titles by Tone
Finnanger, published by
David & Charles, include:

Crafting Springtime Gifts

Crafting Christmas Gifts

Sew Pretty Homestyle

*Sew Pretty Christmas
Homestyle*

Sew Sunny Homestyle

Faces

Eyes: Dip a pin head in black water-based paint (craft paint is fine) and push it against the face. You will get a nice round eye. Dip again for the second eye. On smaller figures like the painted cat, cats on cards, little button-shaped bumblebees and bumblebees on cards, the pin head eyes can be too big, so it is better to draw on smaller eyes with a waterproof pen.

Rosy cheeks: Use a mild red or pink rubber stamping ink pad to make nice rosy cheeks. Add the colour with a dry brush. You could also use some lipstick or blusher (rouge).

Noses for sewn cats and rabbits: Iron interfacing to the reverse side of a piece of fabric in the colour you wish for the nose. Tear the paper away, cut out a little triangle for the nose and iron on to the face.

You can find ink pads and craft paint in craft shops and at some larger book shops.

Mounting figures

If you want a figure to stand you will have to mount it on to a stick, particularly for the bumblebees, cats, bird house, flowers and garden angels.

Make a small hole on the reverse side of the figure and push the stick in. You could also tack (baste) the part of the stick that is outside the figure, see example.

When working on the flowers, just push the stick with some glue on it in between the petals.

Bore a hole in a piece of wood then mount the stick and the figure into it, or place the figure in a flowerpot filled with oasis and cover the oasis with coconut fibre or similar.

Use a glue gun to place something in figure's hands, or to attach the arms to the body.

Garden angels

For pattern see page 57

Instructions

Cut out the parts for body and arms from the pattern. Put the pieces right sides together and sew around. Leave an opening for the arms and a reversing opening, see Figure A. Turn the arms right side out and stuff them before you put them inside the body parts. Sew up the opening for the arms so the arms get attached, see Figure B. Make the dress and the sun hat as shown on pages 8–9. Dress the figure before you glue or sew on the hair and hat.

Wings

Make a bundle of twigs or root threads and tie it together with some wire. Tack (baste) it on to the back of the angel.

Make the decoration in a pot with oasis (see page 5). The bird house is made in wood, see tree houses on page 30. Bore a hole under the bird house for the stick. In addition you need a flower, see page 16, and birds, see page 10.

You will need

- non-elastic skin coloured fabric
- fabric for dress and sun hat (see pages 8–9)
- yarn for the hair
- stuffing
- twigs or root threads and thin wire for the wings

Mounting, see page 5

A

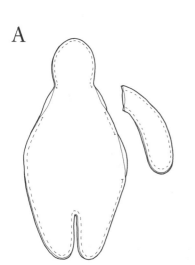

B

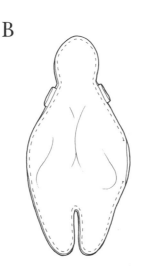

These lovely garden angels hang out in the garden, talking to the flowers and insects and taking care of the things you don't have time to do. Put a couple of garden angels among the potted plants on a windowsill, or make a pretty garland, see pages 8–9.

Dress

For pattern see page 56

In addition to the fabric you will need iron-on interfacing. Cut out the parts for the dress and the pocket from the pattern. Iron the seam allowance along the edges of the pocket, and sew it on to the right side of one of the dress parts, as marked on the pattern, see Figure A. Put the two parts for the dress right sides together and sew around, see Figure B. Cut out some thin strips of interfacing and tear off the paper. Fold in the seam allowance at the bottom of the dress, on the arms and around the neck. Put the interfacing into the folds and iron, see Figure C. Turn the dress right side out and iron again.

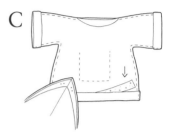

Sun hat

A

B

C

For pattern see page 57

Cut out the parts for the hat using the pattern. Put the parts right sides together and sew around, see Figure A. Turn the hat right side out and iron. Push the piece with the reversing opening into the other part, see Figure B. Fold out the brim and iron, see Figure C.

Make this lovely garland using three garden angels with birds tucked into their pockets and two bird houses. You can find the garden angels on page 6, the birds on page 10 and the bird houses on page 12. Sew the figures together and then sew a small brass ring on to each end to use as hangers.

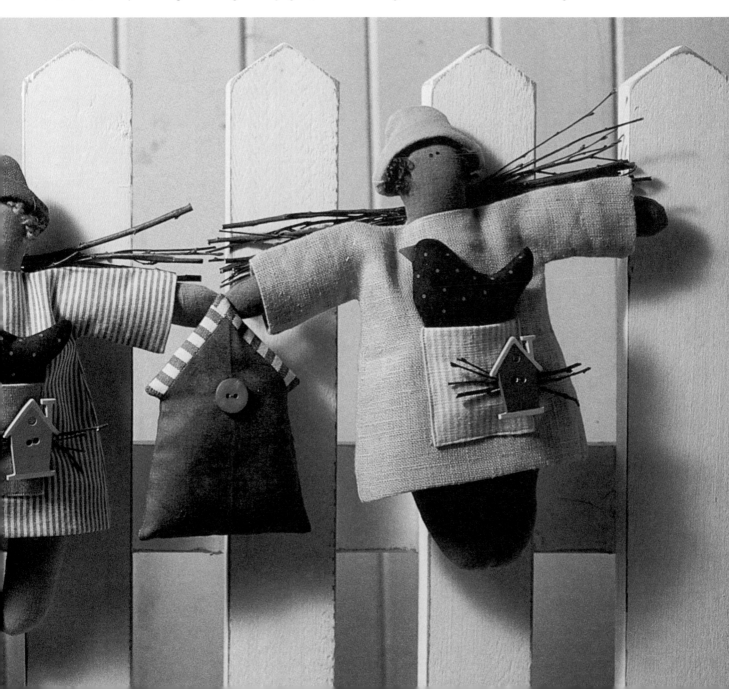

Garden angel wreath

You will need

- willow wreath
  30cm (12in)
- garden angel
  (see page 6)
- seed bag
  (see page 18)
- flower (see page 16)
- fence (see page 24)
- bird (see below)

Instructions

Start with the flower and
the fence, and then glue all
the parts together with a
glue gun.

Bird

For pattern see page 59

You will need

- fabric for body
  and beak
- stuffing

Instructions

Cut out the parts for the body from the pattern. Cut a square
4 x 4cm (1½ x 1½in) for the beak. Fold the fabric for the beak
in two, then fold the corners down sidelong so the middle of the
fabric is shaped as a tip, see Figures A and B. Place the body parts
for the bird right sides together with the beak in between, and sew
around. If the back part of the bird is not going to show, you can
make the reversing opening through one of the fabric layers, see
Figure C. Cut away any superfluous fabric from the beak before
you turn it right side out and stuff it (see page 4).

Bird house

For pattern see page 59

Instructions

Cut out a piece for the house without the roof and two pieces of roof for the front. Cut out the whole house for the back piece. Sew the roof pieces to the house piece so that the border will appear where it's marked on the pattern. Put the front and the back pieces right sides together and sew around, see Figure A. If the bird house is being made for a wreath, sew around the border and make a cut on the back to reverse and stuff it. If it will be mounted on a stick you will have to make the reversing opening in the border seam. Turn the bird house right side out and stuff (see page 4). Glue the button to the front. Make the wreath by wiring bunches of root threads around a straw wreath, see Figure B. Use a pair of scissors to style the wreath as you wish before attaching the figures with a glue gun.

You will need

- fabric for the house
- striped fabric for the roof
- button
- stuffing

Mounting in a pot, see page 5

For a wreath

- straw wreath 30cm (12in)
- root threads
- thin wire
- scissors
- glue gun
- birds (see page 10)

A

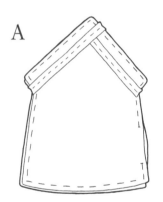

B

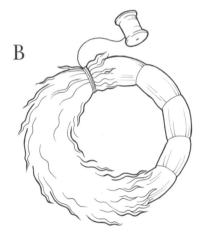

Bumblebees

For pattern see page 58

Instructions

Cut out three pieces of black fabric, one for the head, one for the mid stripe and one for the legs. Then cut out the two pieces for the stripes at the front of the bumblebee. Add a seam allowance to all the parts. Cut out the parts for the arms, and cut out the whole figure in black for the back piece. Sew together the parts for the front side so the stripes appear as they do in the pattern, see Figure A. Use iron-on interfacing to apply the face to the front of the head. Do not add a seam allowance to the face. Put the parts for the body and arms right sides together and sew around, and then use the same method to attach the arms as for garden angels on page 6. Turn the figure right side out and stuff as described on page 4.

Wings

Cut out a piece of metal wire approximately 90cm (35½in) long. Bend each end of the wire into a spiral using pliers. Make a curve at the centre of the wire. Tack (baste) the curve to the back of the figure to attach the wings, see Figure B.

Faces and Mounting figures are described on page 5.

You will need

- fabrics for body and stripes
- fabric and iron-on interfacing for the face
- stuffing
- zinc or other metal wire for the wings
- pliers

A
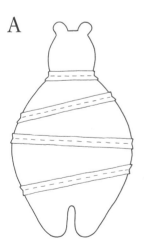

B

There is no summer without chubby little bumblebees buzzing around the backyard searching for nectar. You can keep these out as long as you want to remind you about warm summer days.

Flowers

For pattern see page 61

You will need

- fabric for the centre, leaves and petals
- stuffing
- sticks
- pot
- oasis
- wood fibre or coconut fibre

Instructions

Cut out four pieces for petals and two small centre pieces if you want to make a flower with six petals, or cut out six petals and two large centre pieces if you want a flower with nine petals. Cut out pieces for the leaves as well. Put the parts right sides together and sew around. Make openings through one of the layers of the petals and the centre piece to turn right side out and stuff, see Figure A. For the petals to lie properly, do not put stuffing in the middle. You do not have to close the reversing opening on the petals and

centre piece. Put the petal pieces on top of each other with the reversing openings facing each other. Put the centre piece on top with the reversing opening facing down. Attach with pins, and sew the pieces together with big decorative stitches around the centre piece, see Figure B. Tack (baste) the reverse side of the leaves to the stick and mount the flower as shown on page 5.

A

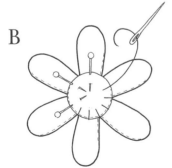

B

If you are going on a summer visit you can take a homemade flower in a pot, or a homemade flower bouquet tied up with a root thread bow. These flowers are easy to sew, and are a pleasant pastime on a rainy day.

17

Fragrant seed bags

For pattern see page 57

A

You will need

- fabric for the bag, flower and border
- button
- iron-on interfacing
- stuffing
- dried lavender or pot pourri for the filling

Instructions

Cut out the borders and the centre piece for the front of the bag, and cut out the whole piece for the back. Sew the borders to each side of the centre piece, so the partition is as shown in the pattern. Appliqué the flower to the centre piece (see Appliqués, page 44). Put the front and back pieces right sides together and sew around, see Figure A. Turn the bag right side out and iron. To make it nice and even, put a piece of stuffing under the front side of the bag before you fill it with dried lavender. Sew the button on to the middle of the flower.

Decorate a willow wreath or similar with seed bags, a small watering can and little pots. Instructions for the birds are on page 10. Glue the pieces to the wreath with a glue gun.

Tapestry seed bags

The backcloth for the tapestry should measure 19 x 45cm (7½ x 17¾in). Cut out the fabric for the backcloth, wadding (batting) to put between the layers and a back piece as described on page 43. The shadows should measure the same size as the seed bags (without seam allowance), and are appliquéd on to the backcloth (see Appliqués, page 44). Make the seed bag pockets the same way as you made the front side of the seed bags, with some extra seam allowance around the border. Iron in the seam allowance and sew the seed bags on just over the shadows, see Figure B. Attach the back piece, and add the border as described on page 45.

B

19

Frogs

For pattern see page 59

Instructions

Cut out the face part from the pattern by following the bottom curve. Then cut out the body part by following the upper curve, see Figure A. Cut out the whole figure as a back piece, and cut out the parts for the arms and legs. Put the curves for the body part and the face part right sides together sew along the top edge, see Figure B. Fold out and put this against the back piece. Attach with pins, see Figure C. Put the parts for the arms and legs right sides together and sew around.

Turn right side out and stuff as described on page 4. Sew around the body and attach the arms in the same way as for the garden angels on page 6. Leave openings for the legs. Turn the body inside out and stuff it. Stuff the lower part of the body lightly with some stuffing and plastic granules or rice. Fold in the seam allowance and gather the openings around the legs, see Figure D. Make the eyes as described on page 5. If desired, you can then dress the frogs in dungarees (see page 22) and give them landing nets (see page 24).

You will need

- fabric for the body
- stuffing
- plastic granules or rice
- dungarees (see page 22)
- landing net (see page 24)

It's nice to decorate the bathroom with frogs. Appliqué dragonflies on to towels and curtains so the frogs can go hunting if they're bored. See Appliqués, pages 42–45.

A
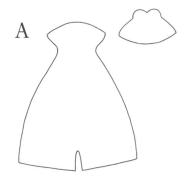

B

C
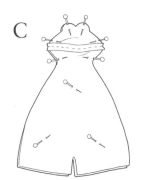

D
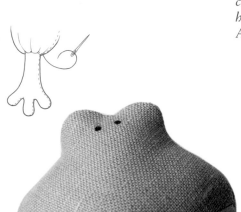

Dragonflies

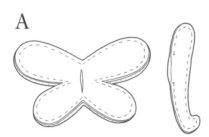

For pattern see page 60

Instructions

Cut out the parts for body and wings, and cut out wadding (batting) for the wings from the pattern. Put the parts right sides together, put the wadding (batting) beneath the wings and sew around. Make a reversing opening through one of the layers of fabric on the wings, see Figure A. Turn the wings and body right side out, stuff the body and iron the wings.

You do not have to close the reversing openings. Glue the wings to under the body with the reversing openings against each other, see Figure B.

You will need

- fabric for body
- fabric for wings
- wadding (batting)
- stuffing

A

B

Dungarees

For pattern see page 56

Cut out the parts for the trousers, and two strips for braces measuring 4 x 14cm (1½ x 5½in) plus seam allowances. Put the parts for the trousers right sides together and fold the strips for the braces in two. Sew around, see Figure A. Fold in the seam allowance around the legs and the opening on top of the trousers.

Iron with interfacing in the same way as for the dress on page 8. Turn the dungarees right sides out and use a stick to turn out the braces. Put the trousers on the figure and fold in two pleats at the front

and back so the trousers are tight. Attach with pins.

Tack (baste) the braces to the inside of the back of the trousers, see Figure B. Attach the braces outside the trousers and sew two buttons in front, see Figure C.

A 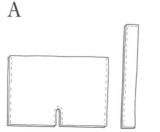 B 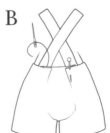 C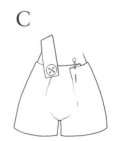

Frog wreath

Instructions

Using a glue gun, glue the fence to the back of the wreath. Then glue on the bow before you glue on the rest of the figures.

Net

For pattern see page 60

Cut out the pieces for the landing net from the pattern. Put them right sides together and sew along the two long sides. Turn the landing net right side out and fold in the seam allowance around the opening. Sew a couple of stitches on the underside of the landing net, and gather it together so it is not pointing straight, or you could glue it straight on to the wreath in pleats. Glue the landing net to the front of a stick, so the stick is on the back and is not showing.

You will need

- willow wreath 30cm (12in)
- frog (see page 20)
- dragonflies (see page 22)
- root threads for bow
- landing net
- fence (see below)

Fence

Use large lolly sticks and cut them into pointed fence posts with a pair of scissors. Glue them on to another lolly stick lying sideways on as a crosspiece. Glue together several lolly sticks if you want a longer fence. Paint the fence in the desired colour. If you want a rustic look, rub the edges with sandpaper.

Snails

For pattern see page 62

You will need

- fabric for body and snail shell
- stuffing
- a piece of wood to glue the snail onto
- root threads for bow

For the snail on wheels you will need

- four wooden wheels
- two sticks
- rope and a wooden ball

Dragonflies see page 22

Instructions

Cut out pieces for the body and snail shell as in the pattern. Put the pieces right sides together and sew around, see Figure A. Turn right side out and stuff, see page 4. It is not necessary to

The snails can either be purely decorative or they can be useful too (see helpful snail, page 28). The snail on wheels brings back memories of old-fashioned toys and would be a lovely gift for a young friend.

sew together the reversing opening on the body part. Iron in the seam allowance along the opening on the snail shell, and attach it over the body with pins. Add extra stuffing between the snail shell and the body if necessary. Tack (baste) the snail shell to the body. Turn the curve of the snail shell inwards and attach, see Figure B. Glue the snail to a piece of wood so it can stand. Add the face as described on page 5.

Snail on wheels

Make two holes the same size as the sticks through the wooden piece. Put a stick through each hole, and attach the wheels on each end with glue. Make a hole in the front of the piece of wood and tie on the rope, then tie the wooden ball to the rope, see Figure C. Attach the snail with glue.

A
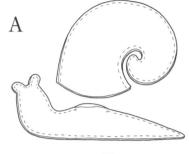

B
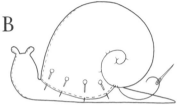

C
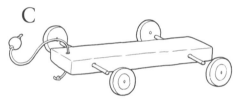

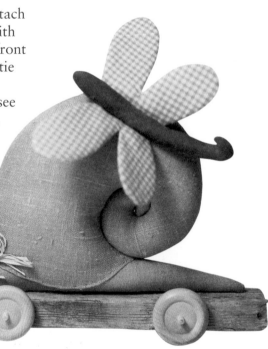

Helpful snail

If you like to relax on the sofa with some needlework, it is nice to have your sewing things to hand. This snail can be used for decoration, to keep your sewing things in or as a gift to friend interested in needlework. The wooden crate and the wheels are from Panduro Hobby (see Suppliers page 64). If you don't have a piece of driftwood you can use a piece of plank.

Instructions

Sew one pillow measuring 6.5 x 9cm (2½ x 3½in) and two pillows measuring 4.5 x 6.5cm (1¾ x 2½in). Turn right side out and stuff. Tack (baste) the pillows to the snail shell. Attach one end of the rope to the snail. You can paint the wooden crate any colour you like and screw on the eyelet screw.

Tie the rope to the eyelet screw and glue the wheels to the wooden crate, see Figure, right. Glue the snail and the wooden crate to the piece of driftwood or plank with a glue gun.

You will need

- snail (see page 26)
- driftwood or plank, approximately 35cm (13¾in) long
- wooden crate, painted if desired
- four wooden wheels
- fabric and stuffing for the pillows
- eyelet screw
- rope

Post

Treehouses

You will need

- planks for the houses, see below
- driftwood pieces or sticks for the roof
- driftwood or wood for the bottom panel
- large lolly sticks for signboard, fence and little bird house
- root threads
- sticks for the cotton reel house
- knobs and hangers for the knob house
- gardening tools, fishbone, heart button, plywood number and letter stencils for the signboard house (all from Panduro Hobby, see page 64)

In addition you need

- a saw, wood cement or contact glue, paint, sandpaper

Decorative wooden houses made of planks are really easy to make, and you can use them for many different things. The post office can also be used as a napkin holder, or you can screw on little hooks and use it as a key holder or a place to hang your jewellery. You can use wooden houses as decoration, see page 6, or as a signboard, see page 33. The sizes don't matter that much, so just use whatever planks you can find around the house, or you could use the measurements given below if you want. You can use letter stencils for the signboards (see page 33) or you can use plywood letters.

Measurements

- **Knob house and doghouse:** approximately 6.5 x 11.5cm (2½ x 4½in)

- **Post office:** approximately 9.5 x 29cm (3¾ x 11½in), bottom panel approximately 5 x 13cm (2 x 5in)

- **Cotton reel house:** approximately 9.5 x 53cm (3¾ x 20¾in)

- **Large signboard house:** approximately 19 x 29cm (7½ x 11½in)

- **Small signboard house:** approximately 9.5 x 18.5cm (3¾ x 7¼in)

- Pieces for the bottom of the signboard house, post office and cotton reel house are approximately 4–5cm (1½–2in) broad

(Instructions continue on the next page)

Instructions

Mark the centre of the plank on one of the short sides, then draw a line from the point and down each side of the plank to make a ridge. Saw the ridge, see Figure A. It doesn't matter if it is not completely even. Measure the desired length of the house and saw off what you don't need, see Figure B. Use sandpaper to smooth the edges and paint the house in a colour of your choice. For a rustic look, sand the edges after you have painted the house. For the cotton reel house make holes with 6–8cm (2⅜–3⅛in) between them. To stop the reels falling off, try to angle the holes downwards, so the sticks are

pointing up slightly. Cut sticks into 4cm (1½in) lengths and glue them into the holes. Nail a hanger on the reverse side of the house before you glue on the knob. Write on the signboard and glue on the bottom panels under the signboard house and cotton reel house. For the post office glue the bottom panel to the front of the house. Make a fence (see page 24) and attach it with glue, see Figure C. Glue on sticks or driftwood as a roof. Make small wreaths out of root threads and attach them together with sewing thread. Cut out little bird houses and signboards from large lolly sticks. Paint and sand the pieces. Glue on little sticks or pieces of driftwood as a roof for the bird houses. Glue on bird houses and signboards before you glue the wreaths to the houses.

This bird house is from Panduro Hobby (see page 64). For ideas on signboards with bumblebees and flowers, see page 50.

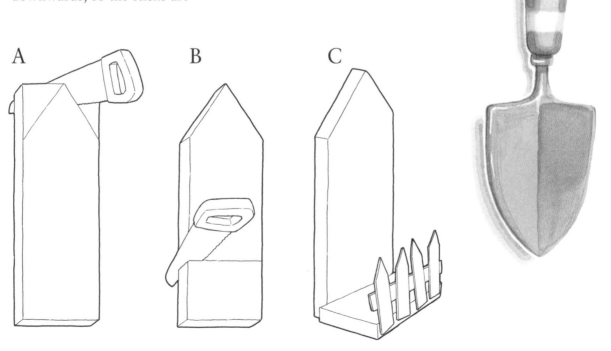

A   B   C

Nina,

Thomas &

Peter Berg

Fido

51

Larsson

Whimsy cats

For pattern see page 62

A

B

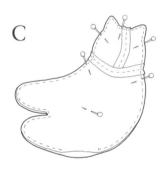

C

Instructions

Cut out two pieces for the head, one by following the right curve, and one by following the left curve, then cut out a piece for the body without head for the front piece, see Figure A. Cut out the whole figure, body and head, for the back piece. Cut out parts for the arms and tail. Put the face parts against each other and sew along the curve, see Figure B. Fold out and sew the head piece to the body piece. Put the piece you have just sewn and the back piece right sides together and sew around, see Figure C. Put the pieces for the arms and tail right sides together and sew all the way around. Make reversing openings through one of the pieces as marked on the pattern. Turn right side out and stuff, see page 4. Attach the arms and tail with buttons.

Mounting figures and Faces, see page 5

You will need

- fabric for the body, animal print (see page 37)
- fabric and iron-on interfacing for nose
- stuffing
- 3 buttons
- birds (see page 10)
- plywood fishbone (from Panduro Hobby, see page 64)

If you want to make a cat with a bird house in a pot, tack (baste) the cat to a stick before you attach the bird house on top.

The bird hunt wreath

You will need

- olive wreath,
  35cm (13¾in) you
  could also use root
  threads, see page 13
- cat (see page 34)
- birds (see page 10)
- bird house
  (see page 12)
- sticks

Instructions

Glue the figures to the
wreath with a glue gun.

*Left: A whimsy cat caught
a bird, but does it know what
to do with it? This is a nice
alternative for a wreath during
summer months. If you can't
get an olive wreath use a
wreath made from root
threads, see page 13.*

Animal print

You can easily paint animal print yourself. Sew together the animals in white or natural-coloured
cotton fabric, before you paint them with animal prints, that way you won't be stopped by
seams. Put some water in a cup and add some water-based craft paint in the colour of your
choice. Mix together and try it on a piece of test fabric. Add more colour if it's too pale. It's
important to try out the colour on a test piece so you can see how much the colour bleeds into
the surface. When painting the stripes, start where the stripes are supposed to be thick, as they
will get naturally thinner when there is less paint on the brush. Ensure you leave enough space
between the stripes or dots to prevent them bleeding into each other.

Bunnies

For pattern see pages 60-61

Instructions

Cut out the three body parts and the parts for the arms and ears from the pattern. Put the two similar pieces right sides together sew around, see Figure A. Fold out and put the piece you have just sewn together against the back piece. Hold the edges together with pins, see Figure B. Sew the arms, turn them right side out and stuff. Sew around the figure and attach the arms in the same was as for the garden angel on page 6. Put the parts for ears right sides together and sew around, see Figure C. Turn the ears right side out and iron. Turn the body right side out and stuff as described on page 4. Tack (baste) the legs together so the rabbit can stand. Wrinkle the ears a little bit at the centre before you sew them on, see Figure D. For the eyes and nose see page 5. For the dress see page 8. For the dungarees see page 22. For the sun hat see page 9. For the carrot see page 40.

These nice bunnies can stand without any help.
See how to paint animal print on page 37.

You will need

- fabric for the body, animal print (see page 37)
- fabric and iron-on interfacing for nose
- stuffing
- fabrics for clothes

A

B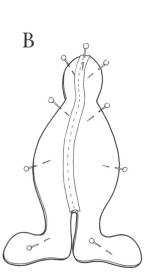

C

D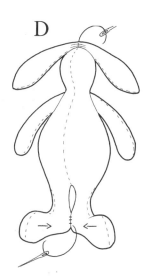

Bunny decoration

You will need

- driftwood or plank, approximately 13 x 24cm (5 x 9½in)
- bunny (see page 38)
- birds (see page 10)
- carrots (see below)
- twigs for trees
- small spade and small bucket
- large lolly sticks for fence and signboard
- small lolly stick and root threads for the carrot signboard
- paint for the signboard and fence

Instructions

Make two holes in the plank for the trees and attach them with glue. Use a strong pair of scissors to cut out fence posts and signboards from large lolly sticks, and cut the carrots from the small lolly sticks. Paint the pieces and sand the edges to get a rustic look. Glue some root threads to the back of each little carrot before you glue them to the signboard. Glue the fence posts to the plank, and glue the signboards with the carrots to one of the trees, see Figure, right. Use a glue gun to glue the bunny with bird and spade, and the bucket with carrots to the plank.

Opposite page: This smart little bunny has got its own little business selling carrots. This is a cosy little decoration, perfect for the kitchen.

Carrot

For pattern see page 60

Instructions

Cut out the pieces for the carrot from the pattern. Put the parts right sides together and sew around, see Figure A. Turn right side out and stuff. Fold in the seam allowance around the opening on the top and sew along the border. Push in some root threads before you gather the opening, see Figure B.

You will need

- fabric
- stuffing
- root threads

A
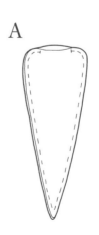

B

Appliqués

For patterns see page 58, for the seed bags pattern see page 57, for the bird house pattern see page 59

You will need

- appliqué fabrics
- iron-on interfacing
- background fabric
- border fabric
- wadding (batting) and back piece (see *Backgrounds* below)

Instructions

Read the whole description (this page and overleaf) before you begin. It's important that the fabrics have been washed to avoid fading later.

Backgrounds
Cut out fabric for the background, wadding (batting) and a back piece for the item you want to make, using the measurements below, see Figure A. If making a cushion cover, sew two parts that overlap each other as a back piece, so that you can get the cushion in and out, see Figure B. You do not need to use wadding (batting) or a back piece for the fleece blanket or the seed bags. If you want to put the appliqués in a frame, cut out the background fabric and wadding (batting) the same size as the frame.

large cushion: 45 x 45cm (18 x 18in)
small cushion: 26 x 36cm (10¼ x 14in)
place mat: 31 x 47cm (12¼ x 18½in)
coaster: 11 x 11cm (4⅜ x 4⅜in)
seed bag: 16 x 30cm (6¼ x 12in) + seam allowance
blanket: whatever size desired

A

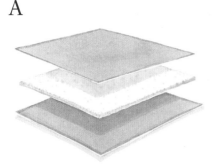

B

Appliqués

Cut out the parts for the bird house with seam allowance, and sew the pieces for the roof to the bird house, see Figure C. Cut out medium sized pieces of fabric for the rest of the appliqués, and cut out iron-on interfacing that fits the pieces of fabric and the bird house. Iron the adhesive side of the interfacing pieces against the reverse side of the fabrics, and pull off the paper. Trace the motif on the fabric and cut out. Cut away the seam allowance around the bird house. If you are applying seed bags, see page 18. Iron on the interfacing and cut away the seam allowance.

Make some coasters with a bird motif. They are lovely to work on and make a nice gift.

Put the wadding (batting) underneath the background fabric for the place mats, coasters and cushions. Place the appliqués on the background and push. Sew around the appliqués with blanket stitch or zigzag on a sewing machine, or you can sew by hand if you want to, see Figure D.

Attach all loose threads on the reverse side, and attach the back piece with pins, see Figure E. Put the pieces for the seed bag right sides together and sew around. Fold in a border at the top approximately 3cm (1⅛in) and sew it to the bag, see Figure F. Turn the bag right side out.

C

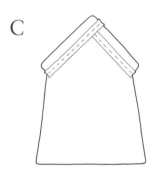

F

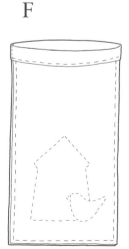

D

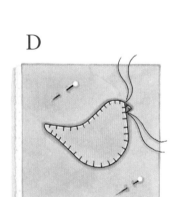

E

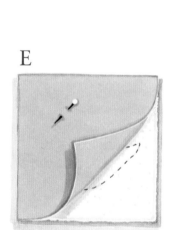

44

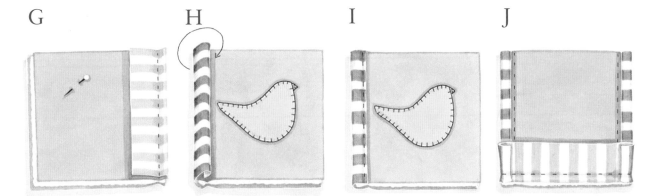

G   H   I   J

Border

Cut out strips of fabric 4cm (1½in) wide. Put the right side of the strip against the reverse side of the item, along one of the edges. Sew approximately 6mm (¼in) in from the edge, see Figure G. Turn the item upside down and fold the strip around the edge and inwards, as shown in Figure H. Sew down, see Figure I. Sew the border on the opposite side in the same way. Add seam allowance to the ends of the last two strips. Fold in the seam allowance before you sew them on to avoid fraying at the corners, see Figure J. If you find this method difficult you could just use normal braid.

Create your own table mats with a selection of summery motifs.

Painted items

For patterns see page 63

Instructions

If you are painting the motif only once or twice I suggest you do it by hand. But if you want to repeat the motif, as in a border, it could be wise to make a stencil (see below).

Backgrounds

Start by painting the background. If you want to use two colours, use masking tape to give a straight line. If you are making a border between two background colours, place masking tape above and below the partition. The space between the taped areas will be the width of the border, see Figure A. First paint the base colour and let it dry. Then paint stripes with a flat brush, see Figure B. Pull off the tape – if some of the paint comes off too, just repair the damage with a thin brush. Make dots in the same way as eyes (page 5), see Figure C.

You will need

- small sharp brush, size 1–2
- flat brush, size 4–6
- your own flat brush for painting, if desired
- large brush for backgrounds
- masking tape
- water-based craft paint
- waterproof pen

For stencilling you will also need

- stencil plastic
- stencil glue
- stipple sponges
- scalpel
- cutting mat (or thick piece of card to cut on)

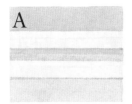

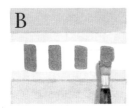

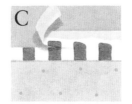

Stencilling

Trace the pattern onto a piece of paper, and put the stencil plastic on top of the paper. It is important to use a cutting mat (or piece of thick card) so that you don't damage the table surface. Cut out each piece from the pattern. If you are making the cat with stripes, cut out the whole figure, without arms and tail, see Figure D. Then cut out the stripes, arms and tail from the pattern on a single piece of stencil plastic, see figure E. Cut out the nose separately.

For the birds, cut out the body on one piece, the beak on another one and so on. Put the stencil against the background and stipple the paint on with a damp sponge. It is important not have too much water on the sponge. Let the paint dry before you continue. You can also stipple light and shadow on the figure before you remove the stencil. If anything is uneven, use the background colour to fix it.

(Instructions continue on the next page)

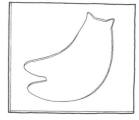

Painted items

Trace the motif onto the background. Start by adding the background colours, such as white for the striped cat, black for the body of the bird, grey shadow for the seed bags and blue wings for the dragonfly. Use a small sharp brush to paint small details and a flat one for larger areas. Trace over any lines that you will need to use again. See Example 1.

Continue by painting the stripes and nose on the cat, the beak on the bird, the background, borders and flower on the seed bag and the body on the dragonfly, see Example 2. If you make a mistake, touch up the damage with the necessary colour.

Paint light and shadow on the figure with a brush that is almost dry. To make a lighter or darker version of the colour on the figure, mix white or black with that colour. Put some colour on the brush and rub it against a piece of paper so that there is only a small amount of colour left on it. Paint the colour on the upper side or the lower side of the figure by moving the brush quickly backwards and forwards. The dark stripes and the light stripes have to be brushed separately. You can draw a decorative border with a waterproof pen and paint a face as described on page 5 if you want to, see Example 3. Varnish the motif, especially if it is going to be used outside.

Bumblebee signboards

Here are some ideas for different signs with bumblebees and flowers. You can try out other ideas as well, there are many different ways you could do it! Half terracotta pots, garden tools, flower signs, watering cans and plywood numbers are all availble from Panduro Hobby (see Suppliers, page 64).

You will need

- Sign in desired size
- Large lolly sticks for fence
- Small lolly sticks for petals
- Buttons: Large bumble bee, head 3cm (1⅛in) and body 6cm (2⅜in). Small bumble bee, head 2.5cm (1in) and body 4 or 5cm (1½ or 2in). Centre for flower, 2.5cm (1in) and sunflower, 3cm (1⅛in)
- Metal wire, 1mm (⅛in) thick for wings and antenna
- Coconut fibre or similar for pots
- Contact glue
- Craft paint, waterproof pen, pliers and sandpaper

50

Instructions

Paint the sign in a colour of your choice. Paint the bumblebees and make faces as described on page 5. Shape the antennae and wings with pliers. Cut the tips of small lolly sticks as petals for the flowers. Cut them so they fit under the button. Paint and sand the edges of the petals and the centre button before you glue on the petals. Make a fence as described on page 24. Sand the edges of the fence and bumblebees with sandpaper if you want a rustic look. Glue all the parts on, draw decorations with a waterproof pen if desired, see picture. You can also glue some coconut fibre in the pots if desired. Be sure to varnish the signboard if it will be hanging outside.

A bumblebee in a half pot can be placed in a frame as a cute summer picture.

51

Cotton and clay insects

You will need

- cotton pulp balls, head 35mm (1⅜in) and body 50mm (2in) (from Panduro Hobby, see page 64)
- modelling clay
- zinc or other metal wire
- water-based craft paint and glue
- stick

In addition you need
- rolling pin, knife, bodkin and pliers

Instructions

Cut a piece from the stick. Attach the head ball to the body ball by pushing the stick into each ball with some glue. If you want the figure to be

A

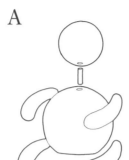

sitting or lying down, use a sharp knife to cut away a piece from the bottom of the body ball.

Use modelling clay to roll arms and legs approximately 1cm (⅜in) thick. Attach them to the figure with some glue, see Figure A. Smooth the joins with your fingers. Roll out some more clay and cut out wings for the dragonfly, one by one, from the pattern, left. Glue the wings to the figure and smooth the edges as before. Make holes in the figure with a bodkin for antennae and bumblebee wings.

Paint the figures with craft paint. Start by painting

B

the body black before you paint the face, stripes or wings. Make eyes and cheeks as described on page 5. Bend the metal wire with pliers into antennae and wings for the bumblebees. Push them into the holes with some glue, see Figure B.

Cards

For patterns see page 63, for bird house pattern see page 59

You will need

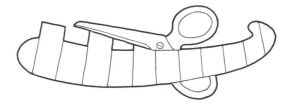

- card in different colours
- small sharp scissors
- glue
- 3D adhesive pads
- pen

Left: It's easy to make your own cards, and always nice to give away something handmade. Here are some ideas for cards with whimsy cats and insects. If you glue on a present or a crown you can use it as a birthday card.

Instructions

Draw out the pieces for the figures one by one on the card of your choice, and then cut out. Glue stripes on the cats, beaks on the birds, faces on the insects and so on. Cut out a strip of paper for stripes on the dragonfly, and cut it into pieces. Glue the pieces to the body before you cut it out, see Figure, above. The striped border is made in the same way. Make faces for the insects and cats as described on page 5. If you want a three-dimensional effect you can build up parts of the motif with 3D adhesive pads. Here I have built up the cats, dragonflies, birds and pots. First, put all the parts for the motif where they are supposed to be. Remove the pieces that you want to build up and glue on the pieces that you want flat on the card. Draw on the wings for the bumblebees and any other decorative lines with a pen before you attach the last parts with the 3D pads.

Patterns

Add seam allowance to all the parts in the pattern, except the patterns for appliqués, painted items and cards. Openings for arms and reversing openings are marked with dotted lines.

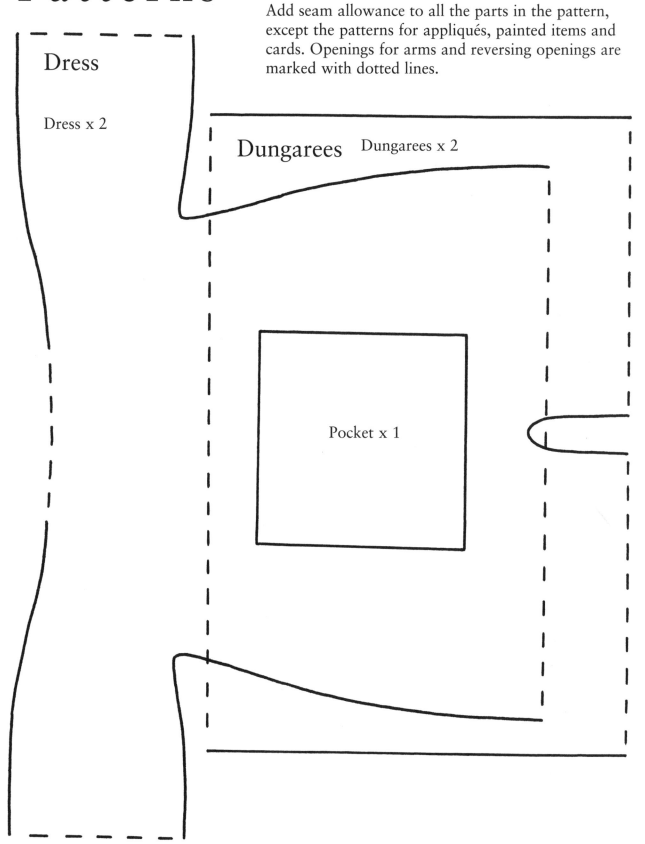

Dress

Dress x 2

Dungarees   Dungarees x 2

Pocket x 1

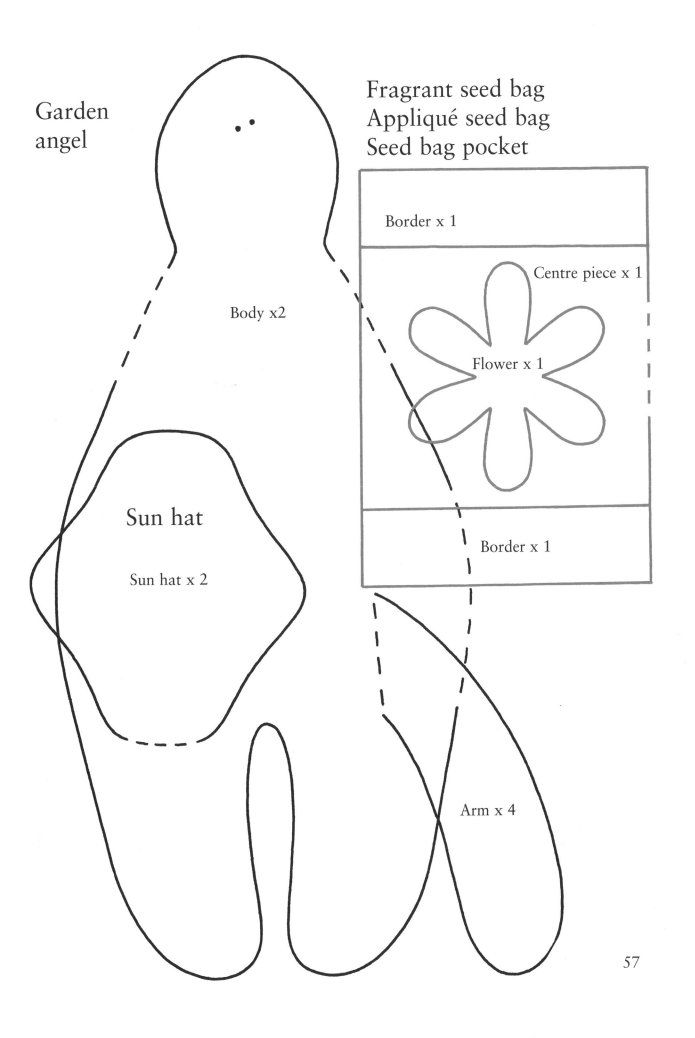

Garden angel

Fragrant seed bag
Appliqué seed bag
Seed bag pocket

Border x 1

Body x2

Centre piece x 1

Flower x 1

Sun hat

Sun hat x 2

Border x 1

Arm x 4

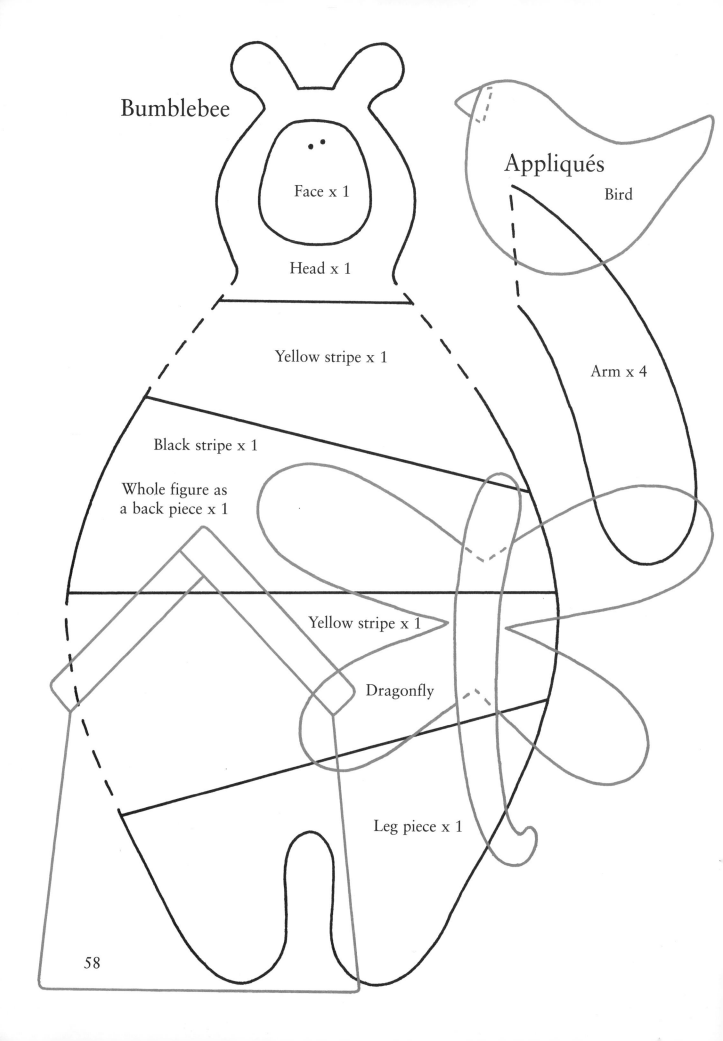

Bumblebee

Appliqués

Bird

Face x 1

Head x 1

Yellow stripe x 1

Arm x 4

Black stripe x 1

Whole figure as
a back piece x 1

Yellow stripe x 1

Dragonfly

Leg piece x 1

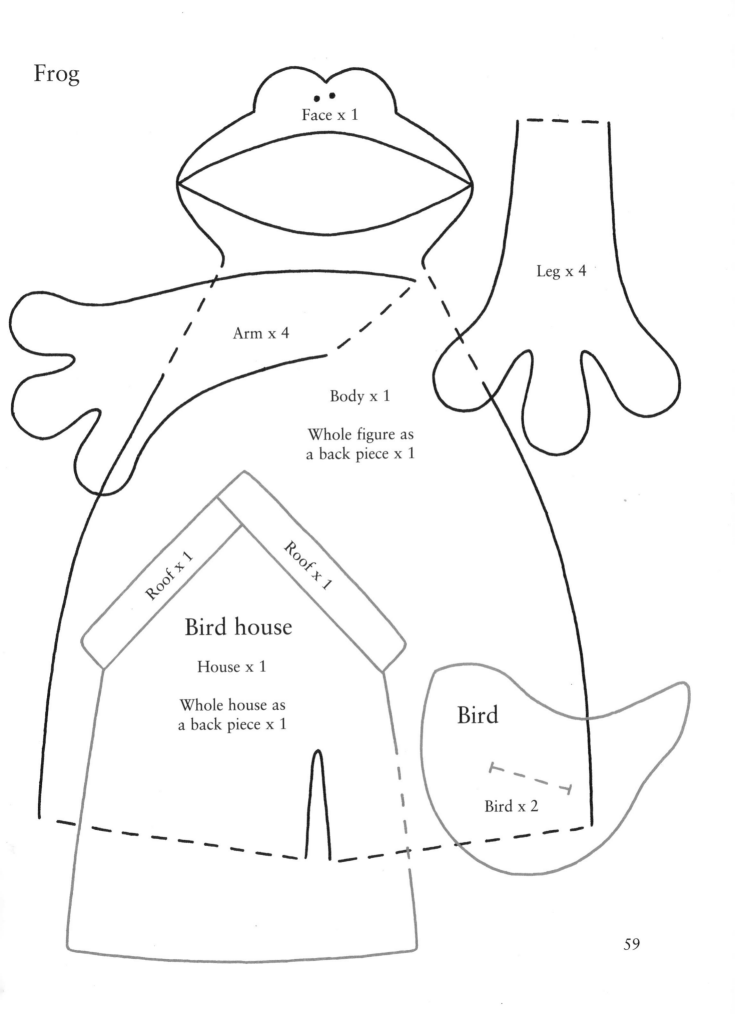

Frog

Face x 1

Leg x 4

Arm x 4

Body x 1

Whole figure as
a back piece x 1

Roof x 1

Roof x 1

Bird house

House x 1

Whole house as
a back piece x 1

Bird

Bird x 2

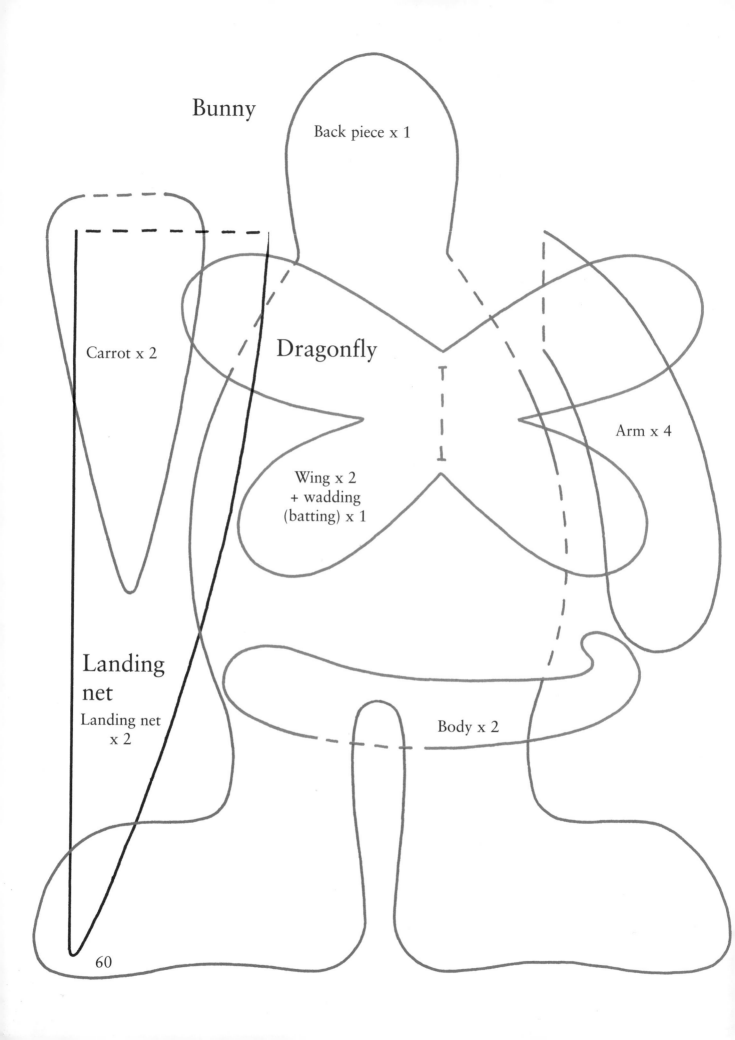

Bunny

Back piece x 1

Carrot x 2

Dragonfly

Wing x 2
+ wadding
(batting) x 1

Arm x 4

Landing
net

Landing net
x 2

Body x 2

60

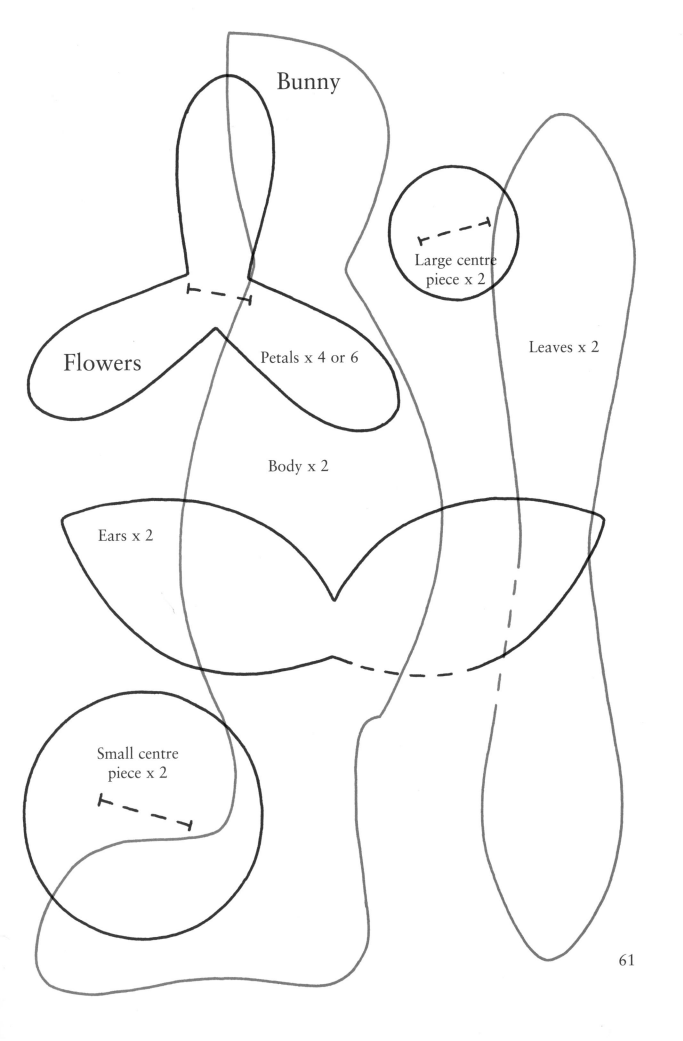

Bunny

Flowers

Petals x 4 or 6

Large centre
piece x 2

Leaves x 2

Body x 2

Ears x 2

Small centre
piece x 2

61

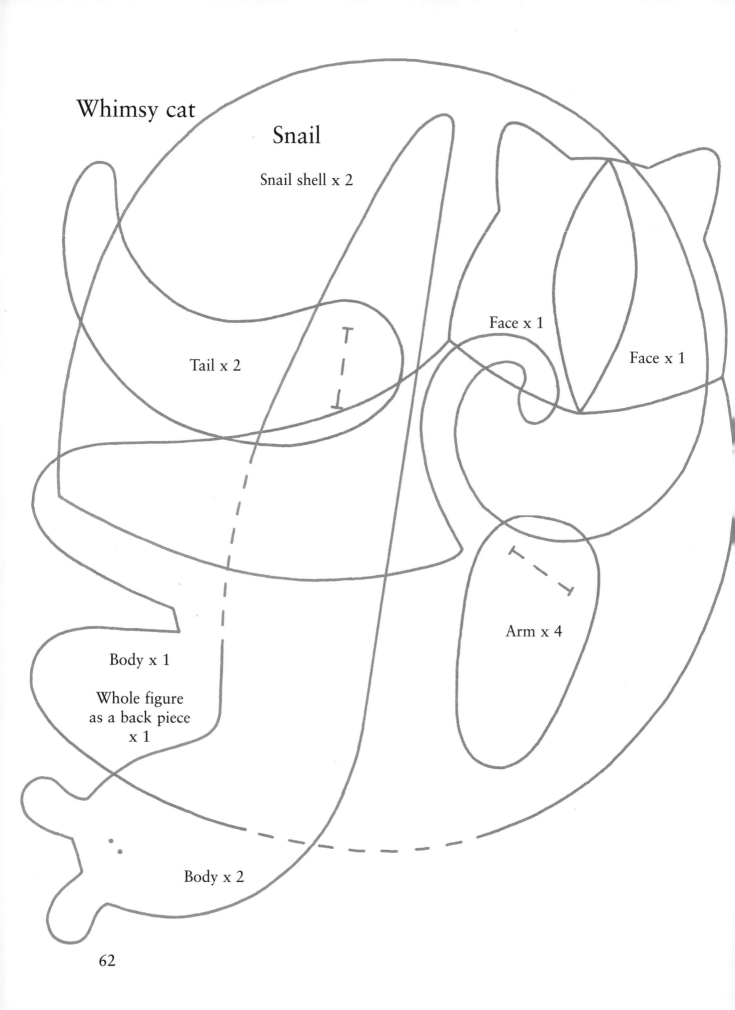

Whimsy cat

Snail

Snail shell x 2

Tail x 2

Face x 1

Face x 1

Arm x 4

Body x 1

Whole figure
as a back piece
x 1

Body x 2